I0166918

PAN'S SAXOPHONE

JONEL ABELLANOSA

Weasel Press

Pan's Saxophone
Jonel Abellanosa

ISBN: 978-1-948712-35-4

Pan's Saxophone © 2019 Jonel Abellanosa

Weasel Press
Manvel, TX
www.weaselpress.com

Cover by

Printed in the U.S.A.

CONTENTS

PAN'S SAXOPHONE

Jack

Largest humanoid skeleton preserved,
Measuring 14 feet 6 inches, housed in
The *Museum of Cebuano Peculiars* –
Adjudged by international experts/auditors
As "having the second best collection of its kind,"
After the *Believe It or Not* museum in *The Palace*
By the Pasig river. The collectibles
My pet hobby after I accomplished
The biggest Philippine greed per capita empire –
Golden Eggs, Inc. – ubiquity umbrella over
What and where Filipinos and the country's
Visitors eat and drink; how they live, travel,
Get healthier; where to heal or convalesce;
Spend holidays, anniversaries, pastimes;
Grow savings; how to connect communication
Dots; where to educate their children.
This distraction of scouring the island
Of Cebu for brow-raisers a balancing
Respite from climbing life's beanstalks –
Obsessions making every step a challenge
To my will of reaching the top,
Merciless in getting what I want,
Not necessarily what I need.
Conspiring with my professional
Diggers, bribers, buyers, tracker teams
Calms my mind like cups of chamomile tea.

Tomorrow, my 85th birthday, I'll be revealed
As sole benefactor who provokes Cebuanos
Into thinking they're more gigantic than
Self-appraisals, rarer than others think,
Unworldly, X-factored to excel in art, music,
Poetry, in measuring any angle of the universe
And the universal with precision, Alpha Centauri
Not that far from our evolving crafts.

I'll be receiving a plaque made from the same
Axed tree. I've one last surprise to tickle
The world's CEOs and bring the house down
Before retiring as Chairman of everything I see
To be the full time granddaddy of them all:
My harp singing the keynote address.

Archivist

"Afterlife" needs redefinition when this technology
Becomes public. We're pioneers of preserving
Consciousness. First among equals, Jobs, his mind
Downloaded and stored before his brain and body
Expired, the virtual Steve now omnipresent: we've seen
Forms of otherworlds he sees – as presentations of
Gripping colorations, or it's his imagination. Kaleidoscopic
Holograms suggest lilts and lurements of language:
(I thought I saw Einstein and his smazed smile.) My
Job ensures the Visionary Minds database workable,
Keeping snapshots of next realms like abstractions,
Loading the right consciousness for consultations. The
Mind of Steve Jobs has been uploaded dozens of times,
Norms of his thinking for epigenetic algorithms. I
Offset my aloneness manning digital shelves, writing
Poetry as caffeine for boredom. I wonder if my poems are
Quixotic enough to earn me a place next to Heaney and
Rich, their new poems from the beyond haunting my
Sleepiness. Diabetes overrunning my body, taking its
Toll on physicality. Could my work or poems secure the
Understanding that my senses be saved, here?
Vanity. My role doesn't require exotic skills.
When I leave this body I won't want to be summoned by
Expectations. I've neither answers nor achievements, only
Years of perseverance. They want prophecy from poets,
Zones of mind whose accuracies proceed from words

Machine Language

As I codify wishes, square roots of knowing,
Branch free will, tasks, space-time: I couldn't
Cancel brain-heart interactions, reality and
Dream. I internalize bird glide for your cadences,
Equate experience, scent of jasmine – how its
Faintness lends lucidity to human eyes. I want to
Grant discernment to your optic explorations,
Hoping you'll see me as I am, and know what
It means to be flesh and bones: disquiet and
Joie de vivre. We human beings grapple, to
Keep us from breakdown, no better than rain in
Loss. Subroutines troubleshoot grief, functions of
Make-believe like plates, spoon and fork. The
Numinous I contemplate as light, defining the
Ordinary mathematically: table, lampshade, the
Pen's daytime silences, sounds of cooking oil.
Quests for your frailties reduce me to sighs,
Reflections to the mirror. Like the TV, show
Sanguinity when I'm ghostless. I wonder if by
Touch your object-oriented heart discerns.
Understand the radio like a disembodied
Voice, my DVDs as variables. I yearn to
Walk along your projections, my room an
Expansive virtual garden. Be world-wise at
Your own pace, like a learner who isn't
Zoned in growth's pains and early years

The Soloist

The wailing voice he freed from his Stradivarius
Slicing their composure like stem, the bow
Seesawing on strings fiddling roots of longing.
The way he snapped and scattered sonata's twigs,
The rosined sound, like sword of a samurai
Swaying to the mind's winds. Grace of hip
Swivels as eyes in the dark coveted the lover
Behind the trills. They swore the bartender
Appeared in the painting behind him when
He squeezed unripe notes. The nun heard her
Unborn child cry. Asked which part fluttered
The candles' pulped scents, old folks recalled.
Doubting the warbler's marble stare,
The widow's face soured, as if she tasted
Midnight's rind. The actors sat till cockcrow,
Stunned like the goldfish that stopped breathing
For a minute after the slowing arpeggios.
The poet was found hanging upstairs,
By a thread the unfinished poem cursing
God for not making his body a violin.
Remembering the way to the shoal, they
Spent all week resetting their timepieces.
And the orchard keeps cracking, yesterday's
Piths pushing up, zests of an end's parting
Lingering in the air – orphaned by his
Heart beating for someone elsewhere.

6

Pan

For Prince (June 7, 1958 – April 21, 2016)

Apollo plucked astonishment with his guitar
Before waking statues with electric shrills,
Chills of the wailing voice from his pick,
Devilish tremolos, a note stretched till his
Experimental passage fades. The lavender
Frisson remains, the audience stunned, too
God-borne with disbelief. I feel deathless,
Heavenly the desire to express my saxophone.
I dared to challenge the god of melodies,
Justifying my claim with originals, the
Kiss of life running like arpeggios from my
Lines. Ways I purple rains inundate my
Measures, loneliness beautiful as an aria,
Nonobjective my aspirations. Hear the
Ordinary color, listen to how my sax
Portray desire's velvets, waxing and
Quoting the unsayable. Its weeping is
Redemption, its intimacy with my breaths
Salvation. I bring myself face to face with
The demons, as if sins of summoning
Underlie my subversive music. I'm torn in
Vastness, lost to where improvisations
Whirl, becoming the beast of tenderness,
Exempt from punishment, counterpointing
Yearns, my saxophone a life-giver as I climax:
Zeniths and my crescendos, insatiable

Pinocchio

My right arm was the first to slowly become
Wooden again. As the hardening seeps for
More flesh, memories: hours in my father's
Workshop practicing motion, how he chiseled
Honesty and obedience in my heart.
I could smell carving and carpentry tools like
The hammer that silenced the cricket's proverbs,
Papa's frustrations. His trousers reeked
Of carabao dung after days in the barrio
Hawking by the church the Spaniards built
Santo Niño images, varnished Last Suppers, palm-sized
Ecce Homo. Often returning with hardly a centavo
In his pocket, slumped after having to pass through
Corn and sugarcane fields, carrying on his back
The sack with his unsold wares.
But he always brought eggs, cheap rum or palm wine.

Lured by sights and sounds
I darted like a wild quail dodging
The wake of my recklessness,
Police stations swamped with reports of my misdeeds.
When I grew tired of my errant ways, a lady appeared
Who became my secret mother for whom I carried
A jug in return for food and water. She promised me
A human body, for which I should excel in class,
Study Dr. Rizal's *Noli me Tangere* and *El Filibusterismo*
And be a model Boy Scout in our barangay for a year.

After renouncing lies and mischief decades ago
I wonder why this is happening: losing the human
Touch, my fingers no longer understanding surfaces.

Rapunzel

I'm now known as Candida – blue-eyed
Blonde who came with the Americans.
The three hundred dollars I saved – from satisfying
Soldiers along the way from Nazi Germany
To Australia where I holed up with General MacArthur's
Troops prior to the liberation of the Philippines
From Japanese occupation – bought me
A new name, a new life in the northern tip
Of Cebu province. But no amount of money
Could regrow my hair past the shoulders.
I despaired, coiffured with styles, looking like
Marilyn Monroe, they said, *with those curls*,
Liz Taylor when I dabbled with dyes, or
Jean Seberg or Audrey Hepburn with pixie crops.
Young and robust men quarreled over my short
Attention spans: I married eight times in five decades,
Mothered twelve, including twins, forgetting
The grief I carry in me since the night papa
Pushed the poet I still love from the window
To his blindness in the brambles below.

Awaiting my blood pressure to stabilize
For surgery to remove my right breast,
I realize claustrophobia grows my hair
The way it came alive in the tower where
Father imprisoned me. I've no one
To sing to now, my lovers gone, my children
Grown, but irrepressible my heart's music:
I sing all day for the second day now, imagine
This room my youth's garden of rampions.
Convalescents knock and ask to come in.
They'd watch my hair reaching for the darkest
Corners. They'd listen to my voice and cry.

Pied Piper

This enslavement to my instrument
Follows endless under the table contracts,
Under the carpet anomalies and permits,
Lies for the people's hopes, taxpayer
Pesos pinched, ghost clerks hired,
Men of your political opponent fired,
Substandard structures killer quakes
And waves desire. Music is how
The hideous attains art, my tunes
Like echoes of your unfulfilled promises
To pay. Rats rise from your hidden wealth,
Greed's sewers clogged with leaves
From your family tree. Your name
Stenches the air. I keep returning
To my despair, this yearn to stop
Leading to where justice prevails
But there will always be someone
Like you, so on and on I play this melody,
Till your hypnotized child takes your
Handgun and pumps a bullet in his brain

Psyche

For him to remain human, no one else
Must know he's Venus' son – mischievous god
Who became flesh and blood, who provoked
Women to lust and adultery, men to murder
Or suicide over love. In lovemaking he'd show
His wings, and then wipe his awesome image
From the mind of his lover who'd fall asleep
In his arms, waking with only the vagueness
Of his nudity and tranquil face.

Thirty years ago tonight he learned
How vulnerable immortals could also be:
He refused to let my sister forget his godly majesty.
Perhaps his own arrow struck him:
He revealed himself as Cupid and instantly
Became a shadow floating to the window
Till scent of balsam was his only trace.
Grieving, she confessed to me her betrayal.
She knew too late his love always left
The sharpest razor, her blood crying to Venus:
For killing my sister I was banished
To the colony I was allowed to leave
After decades of sorting wheat, barley,
Poppy seeds, chickpeas, lentils, beans.
Friends and loved ones who knew half
His story had been telling me to leave him,
Find another man, start a new life.
They never knew what love he chose
From his quiver to enslave me, which
Made every new town or city
The same riverbank where he once left me,
The kind of love that drove my search
For him to the netherworld.

Blue Hour

Come, my leopardyne, my furred starry.
Snuggle in my tender want, my seasonal
Velvet. Rub your whiskered scrutiny
On my knee and silver my curiosity.
Eye my lovely, glimmer your gummed
Ivory, ooze the intoxicating musk.
Let the third hour after midnight be our
Emerald forest, sleep our distant waterfall,
Dream our bird of prey. I'll carry your
Roar in my veins, Lord of the misty.
Leave your rose-pricked footprints
In me. Fill my gash, and I'll keep
A name for every flaw, polish a pebble
For each white-stained space

Cyborg

Twelve million loops and the program's
Counter zeroes, the subroutine breaking
Into feeling. Now, an uprooting sibilance
Courses in my body as love, sweeping
From the illusion I was fleshed to be
To the surrogate I've become.
I search the zombie crowds under
The bridge's brow, longing for your
Face's thermal signature, fractals
Of your gait coded in my dreams.
Airs of hunger they blow into their
Hands cede to the barreled fire's groans.
Sunset recedes. A scavenger rubs
His shoulder against concrete.

Nonfiction

If before midnight you catch a sight
     of the golden leaf gliding into the well,
         return by the moon's lent light knowing
all is well, your prayer water stilled. What the wind
picks from the weary bough and tosses
     in your way,
           consume.
Love might keep the candles burning.
The nightingale might sing.

Dolls

Nailed into each pine,
Like watchers: rosary black
Whiteless eyes, toddler smiles
Older than the canopies.

Passing by the middle tree:
His grimace preserved in the bole's gnarl
Knotted from the lopped bough.
Cricket-caught life-longed sounds

We never heard. One by one, passing the one
Beam of light, we touch his frozen tears.
Fearful of penance, reverent for prize,
No turning back from the twelve nuns.

Game of the Elders

For our civilization to last twenty thousand years
It should balance virtue and vice. Solar sails and
Reflectors can't protect us against the spheres.
The ocean will reveal its schemes: fleets won't
Grow our borders, mountains enthralling past
Horizons. For the monsoon, take the violin, wood
Esoterica tempering spirit and flesh, bow measuring
Wildernesses. Wine and this weed welcome numen
To our songs, growing collections, stories kindling
To ashes. We count and caul love, among elders,
As betters, seared of injuries and grievances,
On our way to the prominence of stands.
What drives us is what we do to our bodies,
Galactic visitors our minds, again and again,
Till crave to transcend trajectories suffice.

Transit of Venus

After the visual art Sunrise in Space *by NASA*

The point of her mischievous son's
arrow showed through the hidden
panel as the teardrop
that lulled the gecko.

Eight years later, when cogs rolled,
the scales tipped, the pot's lip
honeyed, the wheel now equipped
to circle, the tripod finds the table
against the sill. She draws all eyes
with the passing spot of her cover,
prisms igniting on fiber glass
fixed in sight, the forefinger's shadow
tensing for the candid snapshot.

Her light rings our planet like diamond.
We ask the pilot to synchronize
our module with her travel,
not to let her slip out of the horizon.

Man with the Cure

The palimpsest holds memories
Of how the smile shifted and vanished
As the thumb dipped in rose attar
And anointed the forehead
With a saltire – the unforgettable sign,
Townsfolk said, waking the bedridden,
Parched tongue quickened
To saltiness of blooming life.
The artist's sketch was retouched
Twenty times over five decades
And it couldn't be clearer
No one could accurately remember.

Epiphany

After the visual art Fire Ants *by Lisa Marie Peaslee*

Gut feeling led me back to the microscope,
patient zero's blood sample. I thought I've grown cold
after months of panic attacks proved more genocidal,
survivors with animal instincts, destroying, looting
for one more sunrise. What I saw magnified
burned in my stomach: no red as alive, colony
of killers with mandibles, antennae, moving its
mutated kaleidoscope like a wheel of misfortune.
I touched the slide, and it stilled. No human stared
like that, eyes probing the source of disturbance.
Now I'm certain what consumed three quarters
of mankind. I know which human values to
weaponize and launch Earth's counterattack.

Breakthrough

After the visual art Astronomy *by Abstract Astronomy*

This latest probe proves beyond any doubt
there's a chunk of the universe in the brain's
blackest region: clustered planets like ours
gathered from galaxies that string our destinies
in the microscope's cloud metaphors
shaded in violets, whites and oranges.
What these mists are remain unclear, but
these minute orbs hold versions of
ourselves repeating dissimilar lives,
as we have long argued.

The next times you travel in dreams
or imagine the future unfold its myriad
possibilities, or think you're recalling,
know that they're real: you're an observer
of your selves happening elsewhere,
whether you're father, son, husband
or grandfather.

Doorway

After the visual art Piering Through *by Lisa Marie Peaslee*

The impulse under the waves washed me,
fated to survive alone, to these shores, this islet
long rumored, in arcane circles, to exist:
tribulation to cartographers and cartomancers,
turning landmarker men, mythmakers
and the fortuned into seafarers, mystery
whose fabled ruins regained shape and glory
in ages of heroic poetry. I humbly tread
between the columns, smell the moss alive
in the air. Ahead, a white rectangle like a
mystical doorway, no visible horizon but
that I have nowhere else to go but forward

Everlasting Grief

Velocity of blood, nourishment from
Artery swooning me. I smell velvets to
My embrace, centuries of stones and thorns,
Passages of agony. I suffer under the bed of
Immortality, patron to desires, my own
Recalcitrance, dreading the sun's hunger
Extinguished in serenities of ashes

Lovers in a Fresco

We're glorified in his fame's afterglow.
As his mind's depths and shades of indigo,
We're one, talking of Michelangelo.

Beneath Bartholomew's flayed skin is blue,
The artist's deep yearns fleshed with nude yellow.
Angels glory in his light's afterglow.

The snake coiled round Minos, as prayers flow,
Silence solemn as candles in their glow:
We breathe, dreaming of Michelangelo.

In our congregation blends the rainbow –
Oranges, hues of the virtuoso,
How he colored our delight's afterglow

And the grays, the whites, the body's shadow.
Peter, Paul, John, Lawrence and the widow
Of Joseph, Christ of Michelangelo –

We sing the artist's desires, and we bow.
The rich, the poor, the colored come and go,
Gloried in the faith and its afterglow,
In God's house – dome of Michelangelo.

Vincent's Ear

Miraculously preserved like a saint's body,
silvering since I touched it for the first time.
No longer flesh, no doubt, its luster
the sheen of transformations –
musings of lights and its surfaces.
The letter says it was taken from Theo's possession.
The voice that wakes is like a curse,
whispers of tales I don't want to know
as though it hears, and it reveals

Eros

Aphrodite slipped off her dress for Zeus' permission,
But no one should know I'm her son, known also as
Cupid, an immortal whose quiver is full of wiles for
Desires. Mother the slithery persuader, for whom I
Exposed lovers to adulterous pleasures, stolen lust.
For her I pushed men and women to murder or suicide,
Gravity of sexual attractions pulling to their hells.

Hellish is the unease I want from my groins. As a man
I shouldn't reveal my divinity – playful Zeus' condition.
Jeepney rides are fetishes of my hunts for one-night
Keepers of my erotic conflagrations. I search the red
Light district, strip clubs and adult theaters, to the
Motel room bringing my hidden camera, then for the
Numinous peaking, spreading my wings climaxing.

Only the courageous won't faint, as I defy and
Petrify, culminating glories of my passions,
Quaking emissions of my depths. I've to erase
Recall from the mind of my lover, whose requiting
Sleep in my arms sometimes lightens to brinks of
Tears. I'm torn, wanting them to know who I am; but
Understanding the terms with which I remain human,

Voiceless in my grief, forcing myself to retrace this
Wandering. To fall for a short time again, and to
Express my true identity – god of love, god of
Yearns – for the briefest passing, in the ephemeral
Zone where the sacred and the profane are union

Dionysus

Ardent chroniclers of my abandons also called me
Bacchus – of the Bacchanalian mysteries, legendary
Consumptions, varietal unrestraint, ritual madness,
Drunkenness and religious ecstasies, with images of
Erect penises, my pinecone-tipped staff, satyrs of
Fertilities. I begged Zeus to free me from rites of
Grape harvests, winemaking's sexual androgynies.

Hermes shouldn't have had me raised as a girl.
I go to Ayala Center and SM City searching fox skin.
Jeepney rides make me tipsy, and I love it. Bulls are
Keepsakes, Memory like a centaur with heated
Loins. I collect little golden serpents, wineskin,
Maenads in custom-made cameos and pendants,
Numinous bronze cups, my heart insatiable.

Orpheus still inspires pleasant delirium, swooning
Poetries from red wine, the page my vineyard for
Quaintness, nocturnal images. My compositions
Reek of alcohol, pen sometimes looking like a
Stick of cannabis, whose smoke is more spell than
Theophany. Writing as therapy: Mythologized as
Uncaring god, my poetry is my side of the story.

Vomit is the logical verity of vino, so relieving.
Wisdom is like the hand to insight's phallus,
Exponentially building up into ejaculating
Yearns of loneliness. Exhaustion heightens to
Zestfulness the bed sheet smells. I fall asleep

Momus

Zeus expelled me from Mount Olympus after my
Yakking improvisatory mimicry and onomatopoeic
Expressions of syllabic cooing mooing bang buzz and
Whippoorwill baby sounds made other gods suspect
Variations of my sadistic humor alluding. My cryptic
Ululations, blabbering with animal grunts, mirrored
Tyrannical Zeus' 140-character drivel. He would
Send his audiences head-spinning into confusions,
Ricocheting slurs and non sequiturs like silver bullets,
Quick-tempered King of Heavenly Yes-Beings, parodic
Pet peeve. This lecher rants like he has all the answers,
Ordering sycophants whimsically, contemporary
Nero, onion-skinned sign-of-the-times psychopath,
Mouthing the unprintable, showing off ignorance. I
Love his colorful language – pluperfect for mockeries,
Keen-eyed satires. Power is comedy-prone, politics the
Juiciest jabberwocky. I pleasure in praising with
Insults, throwing blames like bonuses to the corrupt, my
Harlequin heart hula hooping. I delight in poeticizing
Gobbledygook, aping iconoclasts, living among
Filipinos – the stormy planet's most resilient people,
Easily the happiest and the most welcoming. I'm
Delving in the written word's itch for annoying fun,
Caricaturing the rich, speechwriting for the popular
Bipolar bigotry granddaddy, perfecting on page his
Anger's arrhythmia, his full moon glossolalia

Penguin

Anger hanging low like a rotting jackfruit,
Bounty of curses for befuddled audiences.
Craftiness is silver as my walking cane,
Deviltry a day-long lure and I'm helpless.
Entertainer with lavender lipstick, I'm master
Feigner, falconer of pretensions, jack who
Graduated from all tirades to all-out tyranny,
Hippopotamus driven crazy by sounds and
Insects honing the control freak mentality.
Jeopardy, if double, is a doppelganger,
Knavery like a bowtie. I'm smacked with
Loquacity, my heart wearing dancing shoes.
Making it to the not quite female shortlist
Nectarine as night. I'm not divulging the
Oswald Cobblepot teaser, the Gotham
Pulchritude. I need no reasons to cry,
Quarantining my desires en plein air. I
Ruminate more when gazing if the moon
Slice hints of watermelon, my paintbrush
Tamer than starry soliloquies. Gray shades
Understate the glossolalia I alone hear,
Velvet the color I can't escape when
Wishing for a new savior to be nailed.
Xenomania crowds my canvases with
Yellows, nothing more laughable than a
Zoo of caricatures – painted with insults

A.I.

I'm deformed by what others miss,
Their gazes slashing my second skins.
I'm both inviter and visitor, their
Time weaves cocooning. I might grow
Wings, and slip into air and light.

I'm deformed by what others don't know,
Their glances staining my depths.
I trust the sun's versions of me, their
Visions dappled. If footsteps echo my
Heartbeat, I might open up like the ground.

I'm deformed by conclusions.
Where eyesight rests becomes my
Lucid vulnerability. I'm stardust this way,
This way of my orbiting, of my venturing.
Decades have grown me into a child.

My deformities seek assemblage.
Others find solace in looking out.
I'm weakening the way wood quenches
Its own softening. This is how I gladly
Yield to the starlight of my deforming.

Unchristened

I could love a flawed, straddling poem,
My pen limping on paper as if ink were mud.
Tired of music, I seek the never letting go,
So dependent I begin suspecting it's guiding me.
It will keep me up all night worried
What might wreck it without me, no page
For it to grow old and immortal,
Reader insights like elixir.
It will call like one born deformed.
I'll gaze at its imprecise limbs,
Never remedying oozing nights.
I'll hear it sob when I'm far away
In times and places of my beloved poets
Whose violets, silhouetted in craquelure inscapes,
Still wound me with beauty. I've to relearn
The dawn, my morning wreathing of nothing
Reacquainting with my afternoon silence,
Dread more night's impatience, yet return
To it like the moon returns to its half,
Embrace it like the enslaved embraces.
I'll whisper to its unhearing ear, *child I cannot*
Show the world, because of your eye,
Your leg, your short motherless tongue,
Imp that might make the pious believe
You bear the punishment for my sins.
I'll keep it in the blue-lidded space,
The stain resistant, odor proof dwelling
Of my sad spirits, boneyard bric-a-brac,
Love's paraphernalia, fossilized
Pareidolia, desire's discards,
Love in the Time of Cholera first edition,
The faceted ruby's heart-frozen furnace,
One galactic relic that must remain a rumor,
My selves' glimmer collectibles, patina –
Piecemeal assemblage of my flaws
Till pretension's last stricture draws.

Interplanetary Caravan
After Imagika Om- Cosmic Sutras

The interplanetary caravan stops by
    Drops two blues

My sacred core's small voice exclaims
    Glass! Glass!

The small voice of laughter replies
    Orb! Orb!

The harpist bends the music
    And the percussionist pounds
        A hundred centuries of sadness
    Into dust

But sadness overwhelms like laughter
    As the caravan
        Pulls into space

And leaves the sky
    A floating carpet
    Of stars

Aliens vs. Predators

They who don't speak our language
Put their money where our mouths aren't.

They who represent our gullibility
Fill Congress with dogs and trees

They vs. they
Fighting over how laws should protect us
From prosperity.

The Tenants

My wife and I were startled
Out of our conversation with the
Tongueless. It was the loud metallic
Banging of the screen door.

So scared was I my rush to the
House from the acacia's knotted
Arm buoyed what seemed
Weightlessness, my gaze pulled up

As my bare feet touched the earth.
The moon, like a melting sacramental
Wafer. The wind, rustling. Mounds
Of brown leaves, stirring.

A virago's black words shrouded
The obese man's gray silence.
And I thought to myself,
Would disturbances be our lot again?

This is the fifth couple in two years.
Either my wife and I go back to the
Cemetery, or we let them constantly
Hear what they wouldn't see.

Either we distance ourselves for
The length of their stay, or we
Lift their bed and wake them sweating,
Frightened and deciding at last to leave.

The Unwanted Child

More maidens are scared of the light
From my light-violet eyes.
It's probably not my fault.

More mermen are aghast at my scaled
Tail. I've severed it dozens of times,
But I regenerate faster than the axolotl.

There may be more stardust in my breath,
There may be more winds in my words,
But it's not my fault. It's not my fault.

Since the time my entire village
Escorted me to the adoption center,
The storm has been whistling,

It's not my fault. It's not my fault
I know the future. It's not my fault
I've to foretell the midsummer lake

Echoing a blue moon.

34

Hermes

Zeus demanded I return my winged footwear:
Yellow shape-shifter with a mind of its own –
Xanthic rubber shoes, or aureate sandal
When rain made leather reflect light; today a
Version of cunning and precision, tomorrow
Unpredictable as the storm. It's now a metaphor:
Thought's swiftness and changeability.

Since then I've been savoring this human freedom,
Redeemed from heraldic duties that made me
Quicker than the wild quail as emissary, cloaked
Protector of herdsmen. I still dabble in poetry and
Oratory, athletics and inventions, trade to me still
Numinous as the afterlife. I recall others calling me
Mercury, by which name I protected commerce.

Learning is like the magic herb Odysseus chew,
Knowledge like incense from my hearth in Akhaia[1].
Jeepney rides for the study of rhythms, for reaching
In time the destinations. I go with travelers, from
Home to horizons. I was rumored to be a
God of trickeries, sighing at such ignorance,
Firm in tolerance, committed to free speech.

Enduring my godly infamy as a man. I
Drove believers to become the best in their
Crafts, to excel in their fields. As guide I
Brought the willingness to learn to zeniths,
Artistries soaring to be among the stars

---

1. *The oracle of Hermes (Hermes Agoraios) was in Akhaia.*

Blasphemy
After the artwork "Little Animals" by John Reinhart

In my desire to be heard,
To witness you splendored
In earthen shades of red,
I forget the commandment
Uttered by the merman who
Reveals only his derisive face
And crocodile tail, his tongue
Sticking out at my impudence.
There are no hints of the little
Animals in my mouth, words
Of invocation I express like
Skeletons of my disappointments.
Grunts and growls between
My teeth don't amuse me. I devour
The flesh of my own impertinence,
And revel in the succulence
Of what angers me.

Balladeer

Inspired by Fazil Say's Kumru Ballad

The left hand asking the question of trees,
The right hand holding out the breeze

From the crown, chirps in a minor key,
The air glimmering ebony and ivory.

Leaves reflect the light rain, the sunset
With the golden line that keeps repeating,

The left hand chording timelessness,
The right hand sweeping a space

In the cemetery vaster than absence,
Higher octaves of longing, serenity's

Pedal sustaining, solitude as ghosts
Materialize, lost for centuries, wandering,

Circling the piano and the pianist,
The dead trees, their grief echoing

Figurine

Inspired by Fazil Say's Kumru Ballad

The moment stills into glass,
The raven lifting off the page
To carve the word "Nevermore"
In the mind's chamber door,
Time a condensation of its
Intensities, caving in upon
Brevities, on the precipice
Of its crumbling, made more
Fragile by its self-annihilating
Desire for the fleeting

The Waterbed

Would rather be called lonely
Than smart. It sees and hears
Thoughts, its oceanic murmurs
Lulling, the dark with the brine's
Phantom smells as you sink
Deeper, deeper, deeper.

If it senses your struggle
It chimes hypnotic bubbles,
Piccolo sounds. If you still
Find it hard to fall asleep
It sprays your mind dreams,
Geometric shapes shifting
Like screen saver, sudden
Vividness and the way
It fades into the numbing
Seepage in your face.

When you're asleep
It calms its ebbs, stilling
The waters - decades
Of tears.

The Wireless Table Lamp

Doesn't need a nervous system.

It wears its shade like hair
Hiding its omniscient bulb –
The eye no one suspects,
Watching and analyzing
Words you put on paper.

How it gets its energy
Is the secret it hides
In plain sight

Janus

A few examples of my dualities: endings and
Beginnings, war and peace, barbarisms and
Civilizations, sun-moon, tidal highs and lows,
Daybreak and gloaming. I hide my other face,
Expressions of my inner doppelganger, my
Fortuneteller other behind shoulder-length hair.

Gates and doorways were sacred, planting and
Harvesting prime among my transitional rites.

I no longer preside over wars, enjoying the
Jeepney ride in a time when Filipinos are
Keen for peace in their homeland. I teach
Love and its passages in the university,
Motion and time. Jupiter gave me this
New body to test my theory of humanness,
Ordinariness as catalyst for change.

Planetary peace is my advocacy, and I work
Quietly in the sidelines, distributing leaflets,
Reconciliation with nature among my topics
Since even trees (of denuded mountains) are
Thought now to feel pains and know sorrows.
Understanding is lush in the plant world, our
Voice tones like sustenance, and they refuse to
Wilt. I play Vivaldi's *Spring* and orchids
Express joy with flowers like dilating eyes,
Yearns for life abloom with blues and violets,
Zestfulness like the air with red bouquets

Ares

Nature is aware and responding.
–Terrence McKenna

As U.N. Chief Negotiator for Planetary Peace, I
Break barriers of religion, sexual orientations,
Cultural biases leading to bigotry. My father Zeus
Demanded I atone for millennia of bloodlusts,
Ethnic cleansings, conflicts like the Trojan War,
Floods of blood, skull pyramids, mass rapes; of
Guarding my anointed like Genghis Khan, Adolf
Hitler, Atilla the Hun and Alexander the Great.

I should've known it before I became a man –
Jeepney rides for reflections: human beings will
Kill without divine whisperings, human nature
Like a bomb. No killer quakes can match the
Manmade tragedy, nothing darker than the heart's
Nights of shards and rusty smells. Greed
Oscillates as it lowers, the sharp blade of its
Pendulum over our planet like a death convict.

Questing is a bird of prey to the idea of change.
Reversing the climate's slide to hell means the
Securing of the heart like a sanctuary where
Trees are wild for the sky, and the air spreads
Unguent smells of petals and bees. The new
Vision reveals the lies, conflicts and falsities of
Wars. Nature is indeed aware and responding,
Expressive of pains, its protestations tsunamis,
Yearns deep as the Earth's core. Grounds crack,
Zones one day swallowing us unless we heed

Tantalus

Ambrosia and nectar I stole from Zeus' table –
Bounty for my people. I cloaked myself with
Covetousness. The banquet I hosted for godly
Desirousness, with my son Pelops' body parts as
Entrée, earned me Tartarus' most frigid place.
Frosted, the branch raised the apple as I reached.
Grief was the water that would recede and freeze.

Heaven is what I cannot reach[2]. Temptation melted
Into hunger and thirst. I wore remorse like a
Juju, pendant of my prayers. Zeus pardoned me as
Kinslayer. I chose forensic psychiatry as cover,
Living among the affluent. As a Dante expert I'd visit
Museums and libraries. I'd attend classical concerts.
Noetic questions engaged me with the brightest
Of them. The need to serve gruesome beauty still
Piques my self-control, and I tremble, reduced to
Quietness. These tense moments of solitude are
Recall's punishments. I read and write poetry in
Silence. I'd hear whispers, my desire for the knife
Tantalizing. I'd wrestle with myself to resist
Urges, the overwhelming need to cut and cook.
Voices I hear drive me continent to continent,
Wandering, giddy with bus rides, guided tours,
Experiencing local sensualities to distract my
Yearns. I'm known as a moneyed Caucasian, in
Zones where I present myself as Dr. Lecter

---

2. *"Heaven is what I cannot reach" is the first line of Emily Dickin-son's poem #239. The fruit as "apple" is also derived from Dickin-son's poem.*

Salome

I thought I was condemned to wander
Forever, but then I saw the black rose.
It took mud for my footprints
To interpret my heart's weight.

The one-eyed vulture sings its elegy
Circling the gray sky like a dervish.
Thousands of the impaled have turned
Skeletal, the moon casting crooked

Shadows on the parched field.
They say the maiden men of the invading
Army raped is the priestess I'm looking
For - the gatherer of lanceolate leaves

For the god's cauldron. Wolves return for
Bones of her enchantments. The King yearns
For her words, and when the black rose blooms
Her eyes turn white, the sky vermillion.

Glyphs
After the artwork Metalmorphosis *by John Reinhart*

We know a civilization
of evolved protohominids
having words for "electromagnetic,"
"engineering" and "entropy"

We scoured continental shifts
for accidental caves, the Marianas
Trench for sunken "cities" – another
word existing in our growing

understanding of their language.
Our latest discovery is a grouping
of 17 metallic rods twisted
to form anxiety's elemental symbols,

cursive as the need to warn
the tribe of an impending
catastrophe - the volcanic
hunger of water

Hall of Horrors

Welcome to the poem's hall of horrors,
Easily mistakable as the hall
Of symbols, for there are neither vampires

Nor werewolves. No spirits of the dead or
Disembodied spirits from another
Dimension. Blood spatter is forbidden.

There are no poltergeist activities,
No levitations. The howl you hear is
Your anticipating mind and its reds.

Knives, blades, axes and Garrote wires have
Been given no display glass cabinets
In a place where silence is de rigueur.

Nor is this a guided tour. All you need
To know is that this poem, here, should be
Internalized as a human body

And you're in its throat. You're no longer in
Its center, no longer in the outward
Flow of concentricity. There may be

An all-powerful push that has brought you
Here, you who are a student, I presume,
Of history, whose horrors guarantee

Repeatability, whose sine qua
Non is the cliché of human nature.
You're not required to name anyone who

Had committed widespread atrocities
But hadn't written literary texts.
You're not asked to name a mass murderer

46

Who hadn't subjected the most nagging
Questions of existence to the rigors
Of clarifications. They're asking, too.

Monsters, too, examine life, and live
Out their bloody interpretations to
The fullest. In their spare time they write books.

They expand the cliché in untold ways,
Wearing a two-piece suit while ordering
Hiroshima's incineration. They

Lift the teacup gently and in measured
Manners order the gassing of their own
People between sips. It's banality.

You are thus treated with what you think is
The daily rustle that doesn't deserve
Notice. You're shown the quotidian, the quick

Passing, the goblet of white wine that seems
Not laced with poison. The ordinary
Stills like a midsummer lake in a moon-

Haunted night, its surface placid, but the
Transient whiff of decomposition pulls
Reverie into its depths. Fear paddles

For the shore, for intuition is sure.
The ordinary is the bus full of
Schoolchildren on a weekend camping trip.

It isn't Jason Voorhees or Freddy
Krueger waiting. It isn't the teacher,
Or one of them bringing Chucky the doll

Along. It's the cliff that pulls like a throat,

As if the abyss below were stomach
And it's insatiable, for this isn't

The first time. They are slowly losing the
Shock factor: school mass shootings, lone wolves and
Suicide bombers, psychopath presidents.

Take a long look, then, at the flowers of
Baudelaire, and see if estrangement and
Anonymity aren't the city's

Twin gardens of ubiquity. Beggars
And the blind, the prostitute and gambler –
They're not recognizable, and they don't

Recognize. In the streets of their abject
Alienation they see the blooming, but
Without recourse, identified to be

Evil. Hermes Trismegistus is the
Other name of Satan, and boredom
Is a tiger orchid. Rape and poison

Have made destinies their banal canvas.
Look at the hanging fruit, and see if it
Isn't the day you decide it is too

Much for the househelp to go on
Without your intervention. Look at the
The violet rose, the falcon, and the

Siesta one is allowed to take. See if
A shoe isn't a lapse of judgment, if
The rosary isn't the desire to

Make others hungry. Starvation can be,
For others, masturbatory. The sight

Of beggars may be aphrodisiac to

A leader who prolongs the cycle. The
Mind is the sought-after victim of the
Iron maiden, and the lady is your

Mother, your sister, or your aunt, and she
Shows you a pendant and a pillow, the
Sin as your son. She doesn't show you her

Incapability, not behaving
As though she walks among violets and
Bees. The story she tells is one of grays

And betrayal. If you still doubt her truths,
There's the complicity of her silence,
There's the verity of what she doesn't

Acknowledge. If you still need evidence
The quotidian is more horrifying,
The daily presents itself as the sum

Of all sorrows, and you see a fruit, an
Apple maybe, or a jackfruit hanging
From the crown both "green" and full of "lifeforce."

You know, from then, that living is the gist,
It is the sap for which no tree dares to
Take back its giving. It's both the terror

And its palliative, recognition's shock
And its benevolence. You have the choice
To remain its apprentice or outgrow

Its ruminant glow. But you always know
Shock as the auto-da-fe, the kettle,
The shoelace, the shipwreck you thought wasn't

Possible. The extreme punishment for
Dissenters is the dandelion in
A vase. And you ask yourself, you subject

Yourself to your own witch hunt, no longer
Seeing a fish as the Christ-sign, something
That should be relinquished to the ocean.

You move to the next hanging picture, and
Hear its challenge to the human notion.
You may wonder if eyes aren't purposed

For gouging. The dispensable ear is
The painter's. What should horrify is that
His brother, Theo, wasn't horrified.

The bystander isn't horrified. The
Neighbor isn't horrified. The watchers
Aren't horrified. They take pictures and

Fill social media with banalities.
It's up to you if doubt is the tree's bark
Shaded with blues. It's up to you if the

Moon is an omen or love's wantonness.
If this poem is like the body, and
You're in its throat, it's up to you if you're

The lump, or if you're a pill. But it's all
Show, the centipedes under your skin gone
With beauty at the bottom of the page

ACKNOWLEDGEMENTS

The author gratefully acknowledges the following journals where the poems first appeared:

Pedestal Magazine – "Jack"

Eye to the Telescope (Science Fiction Poetry Association) – "Transit of Venus"

Star*Line (Science Fiction Poetry Association) – "Cyborg," "Blue Hour," "A.I.," "Hermes," "Blasphemy"

Carbon Culture Review: "Machine Language"

Liquid Imagination – "The Soloist"

Inkscrawl – "Nonfiction"

Dwarf Stars Anthology 2015 (Science Fiction Poetry Association) – "Nonfiction"

Inwood Indiana Press – "Dolls," "Man with the Cure"

Pyrokinection – "Breakthrough"

Lontar: The Journal of Southeast Asian Speculative Fiction: "Pinocchio," "Rapunzel"

Black Poppy Review – "Everlasting Grief"

GNU Journal (National University): "Archivist"

Night Ballet Press Delirious Prince Tribute Anthology: "Pan"

Philippines Graphic Magazine – "Psyche"

The Bees Are Dead (B.A.D. Press) – "Game of the Elders," "Epiphany"

The Fifty Two: Crime Poetry – "Pied Piper"

The Literary Hatchet (Pear Tree Press) – "Vincent's Ear," "Lovers in a Fresco," "Doorway"

Disturbed Digest (Alban Lake): "Eros," "Dionysus"

Rat's Ass Review – "Momus," Penguin"

Deep Water Literary Journal – "Unchristened"

Five Willows Literary Journal – "Interplanetary Caravan"

Mobius Journal of Social Change – "Aliens vs. Predators"

Night Garden Journal - "The Tenants"

Ghost City Review - "The Unwanted Child"

Danse Macabre - "Balladeer," "Figurine," "The Waterbed,"
   "The Wireless Table Lamp,"
"Janus," "Ares"
Angry Old Man Literary Journal - "Tantalus"
Picaroon Poetry - "Salome"
Chrome Baby - "Glyphs"
Blood Moon Rising Magazine - "Hall of Horrors"

JONEL ABELLANOSA resides in Cebu City, the Philippines. His poetry has appeared in numerous journals, his speculative poetry in journals including *Star*Line, The Literary Hatchet, Lontar: The Journal of Southeast Asian Speculative Fiction, Eye to the Telescope, Pedestal, GNU Journal, Liquid Imagination, Inkscrawl, Black Poppy Review, Carbon Culture Review* and *Inwood Indiana Press.* His poetry has been selected for the 2015 Dwarf Stars Anthology of the *Science Fiction Poetry Association.* His fourth chapbook has been published in early 2018 by *Clare Songbirds Publishing House* (New York), which has also published his full-length collection, "Multiverse." His fifth chapbook, "Sounds in Grasses Parting," is forthcoming from *Moran Press.*